AF251126

IMAGINARY CONCERTS:
VOLUME TWO

Live music, what is performed without the posterity of recording, is an experience of the moment that ultimately resides in memory. Due to its very nature as something that is at once ephemeral and subject to lore, concerts reside near—sometimes in—the cultural space of myth. You can always buy that album, but that show? Well, you had to be there. Most music fans grow up with a kind of narrative of what they missed, an absence registered like the terminal incompletion. Be it that renowned artist in the smallest of venues, or those festivals that in time become historic, what we see—as much as what we fail to see—comes to define us. Between these absolutes resides an interstice of pure imagination. And when one compares the numbers of those at any given show with those who somehow remember being there, we get a sense of how culture invokes the mythic. A record can become a classic; a photograph, album cover or even a band logo can be iconic; but a concert—that is legend.

Once we begin to imagine where we have never been and what we have never seen, whether it's Robert Johnson at the crossroads or Jimi Hendrix at Woodstock, we begin to entertain the impossible. This is the game of conjuring that Peter Coffin invites us all to join: hypothetical histories written as concrete poetry of audiovisual synesthesia, memories so perfect in their illusion that they beg to be shared. The genesis of Coffin's poster project began in 2007, with conversations among his creative peers about the kinds of mythic concerts they might each imagine. They took form the following year, significantly, as blanks—simple multicolored backgrounds without any promotional texts—working from the start as a summoning to others, a request to the collective imagination of popular music. Repositories of desire and false memory, these generic templates acted

much the same way that artists from Malevich through Rauschenberg (and beyond to Ad Reinhardt, Agnes Martin, and Robert Ryman) used the white canvas as a screen for viewers to project their own readings and meanings.

The collaboration here, between Peter Coffin and the ideations of the now more than hundred participants who have created their own imaginary concert lineups, is based upon Coffin's conceptual strategy to make posters for these shows into a multi-hued canvas. Reminiscent of 1940s and '50s Color Field painting, in particular the abstractions of Mark Rothko, Peter's faux promotions are in fact based upon the old technique of split fountain (or "rainbow roll") poster printing of yore. Dating back to the 19th century and extremely popular in the early 20th century, split fountain posters proved an inexpensive and easy way for low budget entertainments like carnivals, county fairs, and dance parties to add eye-catching color to their promotions, blending two additional colors to add as many as four to the poster. Since its gradual disappearance in the age of more sophisticated printing techniques, this basic design trope has been so evocative that its revival—from as far back as Robert Masson's 1954 cover for Blaise Cendrar's *L'Or* to the psychedelic covers of the *San Francisco Oracle* in the '60s, and from the posters for the go-go concerts around Washington DC in the '70s to the wryly obtuse split fountain posters by Los Angeles conceptual artist Allen Ruppersberg in the '80s—adds just that perfect patina of nostalgia to *Imaginary Concerts'* evocation of music's mythic past. Look at them and hear their sounds; sometimes the evidence is just as good as being there.

Carlo McCormick, 2017

THE
GRATEFUL
DEAD
WITH
PINK FLOYD
AND A CLOSING ACOUSTIC ACT BY
GUCCI MANE
LIVE AT POMPEII
THIS FALL
SHOW BEGINS AT 4 OR 5PM
42 COLBY POSTER PRINTING CO., 1332 W. 12th Pl., L.A. 90015 (213) 747-5108

KRAFTWERK
BO DIDDLEY
FLYING LOTUS
SPACEMEN 3
★ 10PM ★
Sat 30th February
★ LIVE ★
TEATRO FRU FRU
MEXICO CITY
COLBY POSTER PRINTING CO., 1332 W. 12th Pl. L.A. 90015 (213) 747-5108

AVALANCHE MAGAZINE
PRESENTS
PAULINE
OLIVEROS
with
SPOONIE GEE
HOSTED BY FRAN LEBOWITZ
AT Marie's Crisis Café
in Greenwich Village
AUGUST 23RD 4 PM

THIS IS NOT HERE
Presents
YOKO ONO
& JOHN
LENNON
PLASTIC
ONO BAND
PERFORMING WITH
SEAN LENNON
NUTOPIA
(WHICH IS EVERYWHERE)
ANYTIME
DECEMBER 25TH
2001
42 COLBY POSTER PRINTING CO., 1332 W. 12th Pl., L.A. 90015 (213) 747-5108

de_d - LOOP
PRESENTS
★★★ An Evening of Duos ★★★
TONY CONRAD
LA MONTE YOUNG
ATSUKO TANAKA
KATT BOTH
MARYANNE AMACHER
FLORIAN HECKER
IRA COHEN
WALLACE BERMAN
★ JUNE 20 1967 ★
Dreamland • Louisville • KY
COLBY POSTER PRINTING CO., 1332 W. 12th Pl. L.A. 90015 (213) 747-5108

★ Johnny Bridges Presents ★
NOVEMBER 10
1967
Otis Redding
BOB DYLAN
VAN MORRISON
CIMARRON BALLROOM
WEST 4TH STREET &
DENVER AVENUE
★ Tulsa, Oklahoma ★
COLBY POSTER PRINTING CO., 1332 W. 12th Pl., L.A. 90015 (213) 747-5108

Al Goldstein presents

PEARL JAM

The Butthole Surfers

CIRCLE JERKS

PUSSY RIOT

THE SLITS

You've Got Foetus on Your Breath

FUCK BUTTONS

★★★★★★★★★★★★★★★★★★★★★★★★★★★★★

GAY DAD

ANAL CUNT

THE CHILD MOLESTERS

MIDGET HANDJOB

MC: Lenny Bruce

★★★★★★★★★★★★★★★★★★★★★★★★★★★★★

THE HELLFIRE CLUB

JUNE 9TH

COLBY POSTER PRINTING CO., 1332 W. 12th Pl., L.A. 90015   (213) 747-5108

The Serpentine Galleries present..
NINA SIMONE
AND ROSEMARIE TROCKEL
AT THE SERPENTINE GALLERY
Kensington Gardens
London, W2 3XA
01.01.2000
COLBY POSTER PRINTING CO., 1332 W. 12th Pl. L.A. 90015 (213) 747-5108

★ Chuck Barris presents ★

HI SHERIFFS OF BLUE

FRIGHTWIG

CRASH WORSHIP

FOXY SPIDER

UNDEAD (SF)

Undead (NY)

SATAN FUCK

★ SPOKEN WORD BY JERRY LEE WILLIAMS' LIVER ★

MASTER OF CEREMONIES, ALAN WATTS' HOLOGRAM

THE CHURCH OF THE LITTLE GREEN MAN

SUSPENDED 10,000 FEET ABOVE THE LOWER EAST SIDE

42 COLBY POSTER PRINTING CO., 1332 W. 12th PL, L.A. 90015 (213) 747-5108

TANYA TAGAQ
IN CONCERT WITH
YOKO ONO
BEYOND THE GRAVE
YMA SUMAC
WITH SPECIAL GUEST NICO
Friedhof Grunewald-Forst
★ ★ ★ Berlin ★ ★ ★
03:53 JUNE 16
+49 30 902918570
COLBY POSTER PRINTING CO., 1332 W. 12th Pl. L.A. 90015 (213) 747-5108

SWAP MEET/ LIVE MUSICAL ACTS
RUSSIAN TSARLAG
AND ALBERT DEMUTH
From Rhode Island United States
BAXTER
FROM • SYDNEY • AUSTRALIA
PETE KEMBER
FROM LISBON PORTUGAL
CONTINUOUS LIGHT SHOW
BY GARY PANTER
ON VIEW DELON
CPIT JAZZ SCHOOL
CHRISTCHURCH NEW ZEALAND
+64 3-940 8063
Pre-Halloween Weekend
★ SPECIAL EVENT ★

B.E.T. Presents
FUNKADELIC
ZAPP
TROUBLE FUNK
ONTARIO THEATER
WASHINGTON • DC
8 PM   OCT 31
42 COLBY POSTER PRINTING CO., 1332 W. 12th Pl. L.A. 90015 (213) 747-5108

APOLLOHUIS Presents
ANTHONY BRAXTON
& SYRINX
with special guest
PAUL PANHUYSEN
and
KANARY GRAND BAND
at the Mojave's
INTEGRATRON in Landers,
CALIFORNIA
(near Joshua Tree)
APRIL 19 • 5 AM
COLBY POSTER PRINTING CO., 1332 W. 12th Pl., L.A. 90015 (213) 747-5108

The Egyptian Theatre Presents
Full Moon Christmas Day 24 Hour Concert
NOON DEC 25 77 TO NOON DEC 26 77
THE STOOGES
PLASTIC ONO BAND
THE CONGOS
PINK FLOYD
T.G. SUICIDE
KRAFTWERK
LOVE   TERRY RILEY
LA MONTE YOUNG
CHARLEMAGNE PALESTINE
POPOL VUH
THE INCREDIBLE STRING BAND
HARMONIA
at TELUS SCIENCE DOME
AB CA
42 COLBY POSTER PRINTING CO., 1332 W. 12th Pl., L.A. 90015 (213) 747-5108

RAPPCATS PRESENTS
SUN RA
CAN
EMBRYO
LIVE AT
THE LOST GATES CITY PARK
12 NOON
OCTOBER 24

T.T.F.O. PRESENTS
APHEX TWIN
PERFORMING THE ANALOGUE BUBBLEBATH
+ ANALORD RELEASES
OMAR-S
Ron Morelli
DJ NOBU
★ JAN 1 ★
ALL NIGHT EVENT
TBA DAY BEFORE SHOW

EAT THE LEAF PRODUCTIONS
PRESENTS
APHRODITE'S CHILD
featuring
DEMIS ROUSSOS
with special guests
CLAUDIO SIMONETTI
and
TIA BLAKE
at
THÉÂTRE ANTIQUE D'ORANGE
SEPTEMBER 19 7PM
COLBY POSTER PRINTING CO., 1332 W. 12th Pl. L.A. 90015 (213) 747-5108

JC PENNEY PRESENTS
MEAT PUPPETS
EUGENE CHADBOURNE
STARSHIP BEER
EVAN PARKER
VFW HALL PORTSMOUTH NEW HAMPSHIRE 238 DEER ST
MIDNIGHT
APRIL 14
42 COLBY POSTER PRINTING CO., 1332 W. 12th Pl. L.A. 90015 (213) 747-5108

The Bowery presents
JAMES
BROWN
S.E. ROGIE
DREXCIYA
OCTOBER 23
MIDNITE
Bowery Ballroom
212 260-4700
42 COLBY POSTER PRINTING CO., 1332 W. 12th Pl., L.A. 90015 (213) 747-5108

Tom Hall presents
OREN AMBARCHI
&
STEPHEN O'MALLEY DUO
WITH SPECIAL GUESTS
SECRET BIRDS
TIM HECKER
★ DTLA ★ 8pm ★
1336 S. Grand Ave, Los Angeles 90015
8.18.2011
(the) Handbag Factory
42 COLBY POSTER PRINTING CO., 1332 W. 12th Pl., L.A. 90015 (213) 747-5108

Kiss my face presents
BODY COUNT
DEREK AND THE DOMINOS
CREAM
MILK
SOUP
CRUNCHY LETTUCE
6/6/06
PROVIDENCE CIVIC CENTER
DOORS AT 17:00
42 COLBY POSTER PRINTING CO., 1332 W. 12th Pl. L.A. 90015 (213) 747-5108

OCTOBER 31

THE RIAA PRESENTS

KILLDOZER

AND

RIP RIG

+ PANIC

★ ★ ★ ★ ★ T.A.T.U. ★ ★ ★ ★ ★

Melvin Van Peebles • TONETTA

SUDDEN INFANT • IVOR CUTLER

DOORS 8

SHOW AT 9

APOLLO THEATER

42 COLBY POSTER PRINTING CO., 1332 W. 12th Pl., L.A. 90015 (213) 747-5108

SOCIÉTÉ D'ÉSOTÉRISME MUSICAL PRESENTS
GIACINTO
SCELSI'S
UAXUCTUM
Michel Tabachnik
CONDUCTOR ENSEMBLE
INTERCONTEMPORAIN
DEC 21
2012 11:22 am
AT THE HYPOGEUM

★ Crown Liquor presents ★
PRINCE
AND THE
REVOLUTION
with
King Sunny Ade
and Queen Latifah
DJ SET KING TUBBY
At the Royal Albert Hall
HIGH NOON JANUARY 1
★ +44 20 7589 8212 ★
COLBY POSTER PRINTING CO., 1332 W. 12th Pl., L.A. 90015 (213) 747-5108

J. DIAMOND PRESENTS
CHIC
IMAGINATION
KASHIF
MR. FINGERS
ON THE DECKS
AT THE
MUSIC BOX
CHICAGO
3733 N Southport Ave,
Chicago, IL 60613
FEB 28TH 9PM
COLBY POSTER PRINTING CO., 1332 W. 12th Pl., L.A. 90015 (213) 747-5108

★ ONE NIGHT STAND! ★

AN EARLY SET AND A LATE SET WITH

SAM COOKE

WITH HIS BAND CORNELL DUPREE

MARCH 12TH

with

ALBERT "GENTLEMAN JUNE" GARDNER
★ TATE HOUSTON ★ KING CURTIS ★
★ JIMMY LEWIS ★ GEORGE STUBBS ★
★ & CLIFTON WHITE ★

AFTER DANCE PARTY WITH

BRIAN DEGRAW • SPENCER SWEENEY
AND DJ TRUMASTR

Frank's Cocktail Lounge,
660 Fulton Street Brooklyn NY 11217

SAFE GALLERY PRESENTS
an extended evening raga of the Misfits'
HALLOWEEN
as performed by
GLENN DANZIG ★ JERRY GARCIA
SONNY SHARROCK ★ MARY TIMONY
& RICK BISHOP
LIVE
AT THE MOUTH OF THE CARLSBAD CAVERNS
OCTOBER 31st AT DUSK
AS A SPIRALING STREAM OF BATS
ASCEND INTO
THE DARKENING SKY.
COLBY POSTER PRINTING CO., 1332 W. 12th Pl., L.A. 90015 (213) 747-5108

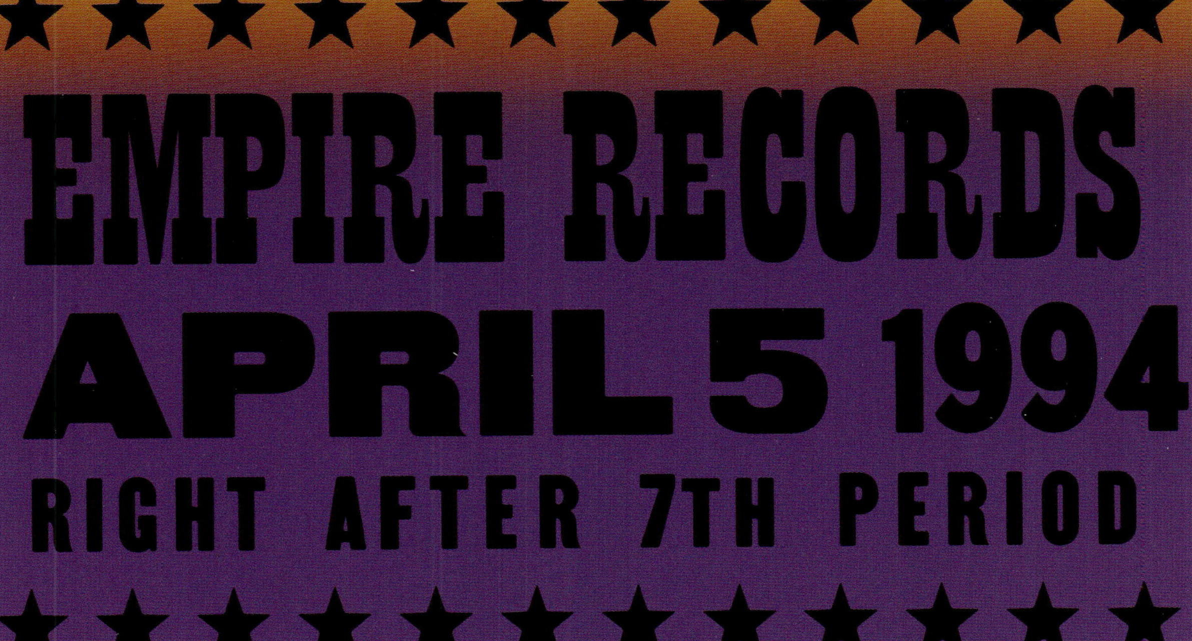
DJ DAVID SILVER PRESENTS
MYSTIK SPIRAL
CRUCIAL TAUNT
JESSE AND THE RIPPERS
ZACK ATTACK
FT: JESSIE SPANO
MISSION CONTROL
EMPIRE RECORDS
APRIL 5 1994
RIGHT AFTER 7TH PERIOD
COLBY POSTER PRINTING CO., 1332 W. 12th PL, L.A. 90015 (213) 747-5108

SITUATIONS presents
UNIVERSE
FEATURING
YMA SUMAC
GOOGOOSH
NENEH CHERRY
CHAKA KHAN
LUZMILA CARPIO
AND AN OPENING PERFORMANCE BY
KLYMAXX
"Meeting in the Ladies Room"
& NASTIE BAND
November 11 11PM
MAGIC STICK
4120 Woodward Ave Detroit MI
COLBY POSTER PRINTING CO., 1332 W. 12th Pl., L.A. 90015 (213) 747-5108

2001 ODYSSEY CLUB
PRESENTS
BROOKLYN EXPRESS
CROWN HEIGHTS AFFAIR
CROSS BRONX EXPRESSWAY
HARLEM WORLD CREW
& THE MANHATTANS
WITH SPECIAL GUESTS THE B.B.&Q. BAND
★ ROCK ★ SKATE ★ ROLL ★ BOUNCE ★
$6 SATURDAY MATINEE
ROLLERJAM USA
STATEN ISLAND, N.Y.
42 COLBY POSTER PRINTING CO., 1332 W. 12th Pl., L.A. 90015 (213) 747-5108

DANIELE BALDELLI & DINO DE LAURENTIIS
KINDLY REQUEST YOUR PRESENCE AT
THE END OF
THE WORLD
FEATURING
BAGARRE
B.W.H.   CASCO
KANO   MARCOS VALLE
RYAN PARIS & SCOTCH
WITH SPECIAL GIORGIOS
ARMANI & MORODER
AND THE FABULOUS
AMANDA LEAR
NEW YEARS EVE
BAIA DEGLI ANGELI
Via Panoramica, 36, 61011
Gabicce Mare
COLBY POSTER PRINTING CO., 1332 W. 12th Pl. L.A. 90015 (213) 747-5108

THE N.Y. SANITATION DEPARTMENT PRESENTS
** WORLD WAR III **
THE WORLD FAMOUS SUPREME TEAM
— VS —
THE WORLD CLASS WRECKIN' CRU
— VS —
THE WORLD WRESTLING FEDERATION SUPERSTARS
WORLD PREMIERE
PAY-PER-VIEW EVENT
JAN. 20TH 1985
LIVE FROM
THE WORLD MARTIAL ARTS ARTS CENTER
540 Atlantic Avenue, 3rd Floor
Brooklyn, NY
CONTACT YOUR LOCAL CABLE PROVIDER
COLBY POSTER PRINTING CO., 1332 W. 12th Pl., L.A. 90015 (213) 747-5108

BOB JAMES
PIANO QUARTET
★ FEATURING ★
LANG LANG
YUJA WANG
MIKE LANG
★ ALSO FEATURING ★
THE PIANO GUYS
INTRODUCTIONS BY K.D. LANG
LIVE AT THE SAN FRANCISCO
JAZZ CENTER
APRIL 1 • 4PM
COLBY POSTER PRINTING CO. 1332 W. 12th Pl., L.A. 90015 (213) 747-5108

CARLO PONTI PRESENTS
ELSTON GUNNN
TEDHAM PORTERHOUSE
BLIND BOY GRUNT
ROBERT MILKWOOD THOMAS
LUCKY WILBURY
JUNE 1
THE ASTRODOME
HOUSTON, TEXAS
COLBY POSTER PRINTING CO., 1332 W. 12th Pl., L.A. 90015 (213) 747-5108

SIMULTANEOUS CONCERT IN BLUE

★ featuring ★

GYÖRGY LIGETI'S POÈME SYMPHONIQUE FOR 100 METRONOMES

PETER HAMBURGER'S 18 RAINDROP MACHINES

5 CYMBALISTS FROM BREAD & PUPPET'S INSURRECTION ORATORIO

GLENN GOULD PERFORMING BACH'S GOLDBERG VARIATIONS

SUNDAY 7pm JUNE 3 2018

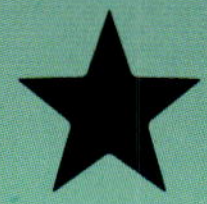 in the Paper-Mâché Cathedral at Bread & Puppet, Glover, VT 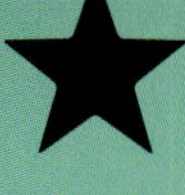

AUGUST 13TH
AT MIDNIGHT
WITCH SEASON
PRODUCTIONS PRESENTS
FAIRPORT CONVENTION
AND THE EVERLY BROTHERS
MARY TIMONY &
LINDA MARTELL
MEYERHOFF SYMPHONY HALL, BALTIMORE MD
410 783-8000

SOFT CELL
AND
CESÁRIA ÉVORA
DJ FRANKIE KNUCKLES
Stage design and light show
by James Turrell
PERFORMING AT
CONFORT MODERNE
85 Rue du Faubourg du Pont Neuf,
86000 Poitiers, France
+33 5 49 46 08 08
COLBY POSTER PRINTING CO., 1332 W. 12th PL, L.A. 90015 (213) 747-5108

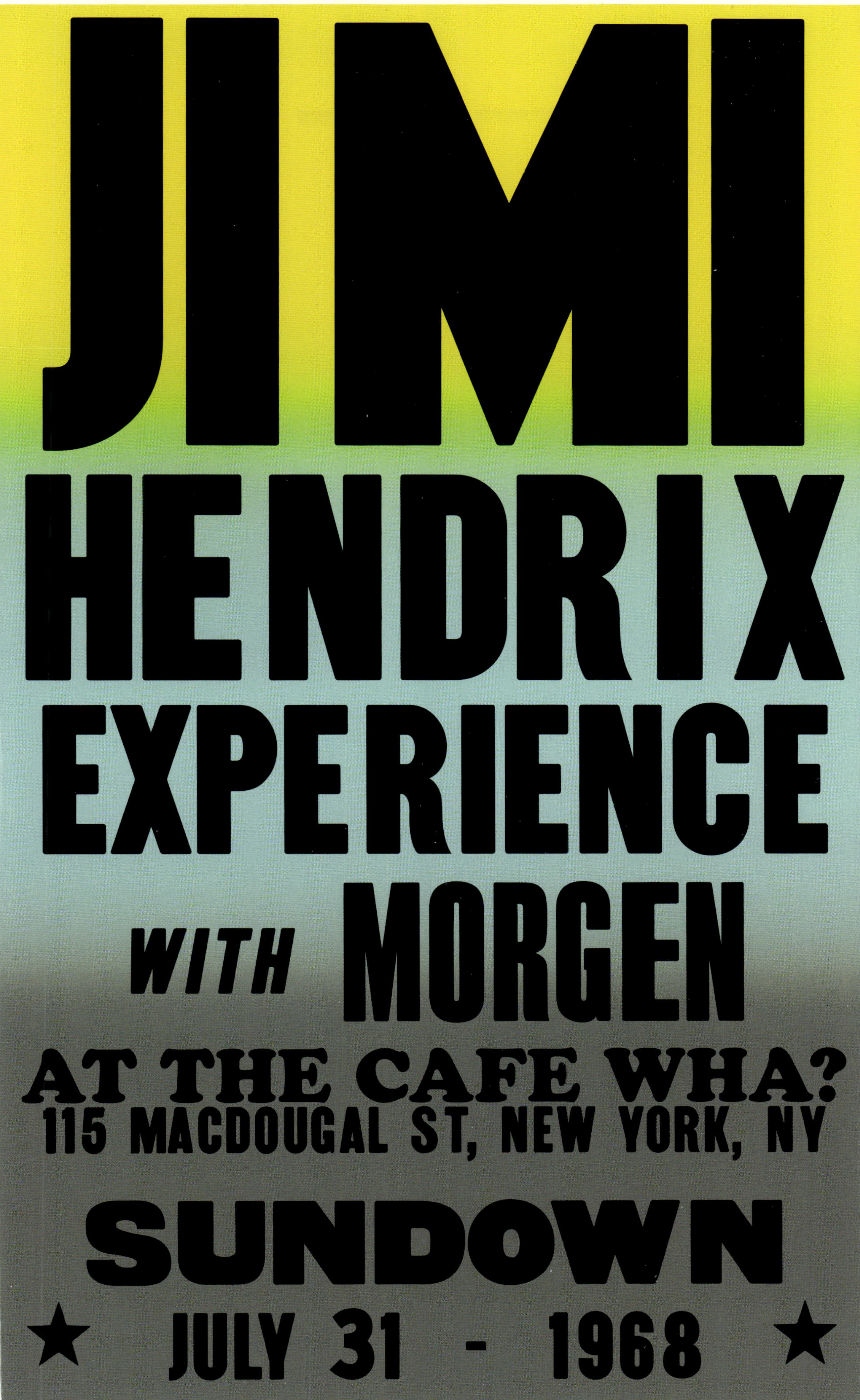

JIMI
HENDRIX
EXPERIENCE
WITH MORGEN
AT THE CAFE WHA?
115 MACDOUGAL ST, NEW YORK, NY
SUNDOWN
★ JULY 31 - 1968 ★
COLBY POSTER PRINTING CO., 1332 W. 12th Pl. L.A. 90015 (213) 747-5108

★★★★★ ★★ The American Tour ★★ ★★★★★
PRINCE
RIHANNA
PUBLIC ENEMY
★ WITH SPECIAL GUESTS ★
JANELLE MONÁE ★ JESSICA CARE MOORE
SPECIAL APPEARANCES BY
★ COMMON & JOHN LEGEND ★ LOS LOBOS ★
★ CALLE 13 ★ INDIGO GIRLS ★
★ TALIB KWELI ★
★ BRUCE SPRINGSTEEN & TOM MORELLO ★
ALL SHOWS FREE AND OPEN TO THE PUBLIC
NORTH CHARLESTON, SC - SANFORD, FL - FERGUSON, MO - STATEN
ISLAND, NY, BALTIMORE, MD - BEAVERCREEK, OH - MCKINNEY, TX —
MORE CITIES TO COME • DOCUMENTARY PHOTOGRAPHY BY GORDON
PARKS, CHARLES MOORE, AND MANY OTHERS
42 COLBY POSTER PRINTING CO., 1332 W. 12th Pl., L.A. 90015 (213) 747-5108

LYDIA LUNCH PRESENTS
EARTHA KITT
★ ★
BETTY DAVIS
YVONNE FAIR
Sylvia Black
& CELLULAR CHAOS
October 31 8pm
★ The Apollo ★
253 W 125th St, N.Y.C.
212 531-5300
42 COLBY POSTER PRINTING CO., 1332 W. 12th Pl, LA 90015 (213) 747-5108

THE BOK KAI TEMPLE APPRECIATION CLUB PRESENTS
DANIELLE DAX
THE MELVINS, WITH GUEST BRITTANY HOWARD
AMY DENIO
MUSLIMGAUZE
LaDONNA SMITH
HOSTED BY KCMU'S DAMON CREED
MAY, 1 8pm
THE CROCODILE CAFE
2ND AVE & BLANCHARD, SEATTLE
42 COLBY POSTER PRINTING CO., 1332 W. 12th Pl., L.A. 90015 (213) 747-5108

NANCY CUNARD PRESENTS
LA LUPE
★ ALSO FEATURING ★
LIZZIE MERCIER DESCLOUX
WITH SPECIAL GUEST
SATIE
★ SUNDAY ★
OCTOBER 31
13:00PM
ISADORA DUNCAN DANCE
RESEARCH CENTER
CHRISAFIS 34
VIRONAS 162 32
21 0762 1234

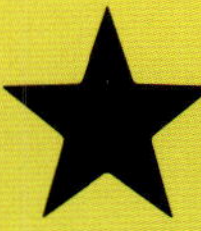
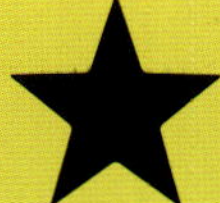

★★★★★★★ Terry Allen presents ★★★★★★★
DOLLY PARTON
THE BUTTHOLE SURFERS
STUBB'S BAR-B-Q
801 RED RIVER AUSTIN, TEXAS
MAY 5TH 9PM

THE ROACHES
TARA JANE ONEIL
JONI MITCHELL
KLAUS NOMI
SOILED MATTRESS
& THE SPRINGS
ELIZABETH COTTEN WITH A
GRAND DAUGHTER SINGING
SPLIT ME WIDE OPEN
IN AN UNDERGROUND CLUB
YOU GET THERE BY DROWNING OR NOT DROWNING
RATHER, WHEN YOU GET SUCKED UNDER
THE RHINE BY A WHIRLPOOL
★ CLUB IS UNDER RIVER ★
NO ONE TURNED AWAY FOR LACK OF MONEY OR GLAMOR
RIGHT NOW
EAT THE RICH GETS YOU IN FOR FREE
COLBY POSTER PRINTING CO., 1332 W. 12th Pl. L.A. 90015 (213) 747-5108

BOB MARLEY
& THE WAILERS
FELA KUTI
THE CLASH
E S G
MADISON SQUARE GARDEN
NEW YORK
OCT 3, 1980
COLBY POSTER PRINTING CO., 1332 W. 12th Pl., L.A. 90015 (213) 747-5108

THE CITY OF SAN FRANCISCO PRESENTS
SUN RA
ARKESTRA
THE BLUE HUMANS
FEATURING
★ RUDOLPH GREY ★ ALAN LIGHT ★ BEAVER HARRIS ★
★ ARTHUR DOYLE ★ TOM SURGAL & JIM SAUTER ★
SKELETON CREW
FEATURING
FRED FRITH & TOM CORA
GOLDEN GATE PARK
July 4 NOON

宇宙天王
AKA EMPEROR
OF THE UNIVERSE
& KRAFTWERK
YOUNG-AE KIM
FEATURING MALCOLM MCLAREN
PERFORMING SELECTED ARIAS
FROM MADAME BUTTERFLY
BENJAMIN CHO
PERFORMING THE BACH CELLO SUITES 4, 5, AND 1
East River Amphitheater
NOV 24 16:03
42 COLBY POSTER PRINTING CO., 1332 W. 12th Pl., L.A. 90015 (213) 747-5108

★★★ INFORMAL NATION PRESENTS ★★★
PUBLIC ENEMY
PLAYING WITH MEMBERS OF ANTHRAX
FISHBONE
THE MO'FESSIONALS
GROOVE SHOP
DNA LOUNGE, SF
SUNDAY MAY 30TH
Doors at 8pm $10 21+
HOSTED BY THE PIRATE DJS
CULBY POSTER PRINTING CO., 1332 W. 12th Pl., L.A. 90015 (213) 747-5108

ZOMBOCOMBO PRESENTS
FELA RANSOME KUTI & THE AFRICA 70
JAMES BROWN & THE JB'S FEATURING LYN COLLINS
SLY & THE FAMILY STONE
CAN
JACO PASTORIUS
ROBERT JOHNSON
ZEBULON
W258 WYTHE AVENUE
BROOKLYN NY
COLBY POSTER PRINTING CO 1332 W 17th PL. L.A. 90015 (213) 747-5108

TUESDAY JANUARY 2
SCIENCE FICTION DAY
8 PM TO 2 AM
UTOPIAN PRODUCTIONS PRESENTS
A DREAM CONCERT WITH
★ LÉON ★
THEREMIN
and
★ LAURIE ★
ANDERSON
ALSO CONSTANCE DEMBY
& TANGERINE DREAM
LIVE AT THE ALBERT EINSTEIN PLANETARIUM
INDEPENDENCE AVE AT 6TH ST SW
WASHINGTON D.C.
COLBY POSTER PRINTING CO., 1332 W. 12th Pl., L.A. 90015 (213) 747-5108

CHET HELMS PRESENTS IN DENVER
Nov 18 & 19
DOORS OPEN AT 7:45PM
COLLECTORS
BUBBLE PUPPY
BOENZEE
CRYQUE
MYSTERY TREND
THE FAMILY DOG
1601 WEST EVANS
MUST BE 18 TO ENTER
COLBY POSTER PRINTING CO., 1332 W. 12th Pl. L.A. 90015 (213) 747-5108

CRASH WORSHIP
DISPOSABLE HEROES
OF HIPHOPRISY
*** L7 ***
SOUP DRAGONS
TREEPEOPLE
★ COLORADO COLLEGE ★
FINE ARTS CENTER 1990
8 PM SHARP
COLBY POSTER PRINTING CO., 1332 W. 12th Pl., L.A. 90015 (213) 747-5108

THE LAST POETS
TONY CONRAD
SUICIDE
DAVID BOWIE
THE POETICS
SECRET LOCATION IN LA
★ January 10 ★ January 31 ★
SECRET LOCATION NYC
★ April 9 ★ May 27 ★ July 16 ★
42 COLBY POSTER PRINTING CO., 1332 W. 12th PL. L.A. 90015 (213) 747-5108

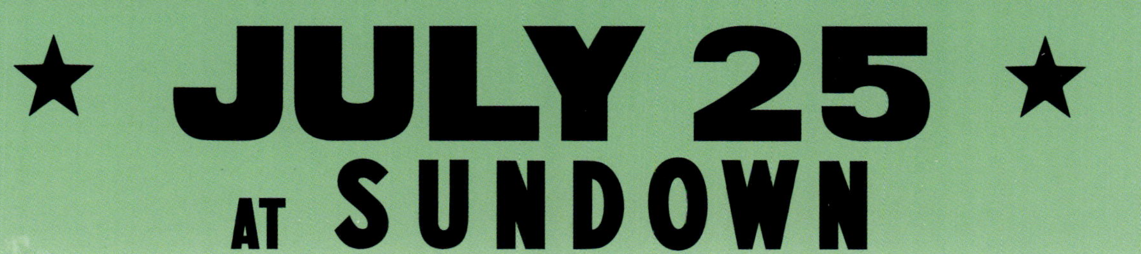
★ PERFORMING LIVE ★
HONEY
BADGERS
& PRINCE
With a poetry reading by Bernadette Mayer
AT THE
ASHFIELD LAKE HOUSE
★ JULY 25 ★
AT SUNDOWN
42 COLBY POSTER PRINTING CO., 1332 W. 12th Pl. L.A. 9001* (213) 747-5108

LE PÉTOMANE
CHARLIE PATTON
RICK JAMES &
NEIL YOUNG'S BAND
SANDY DENNY
BETTY DAVIS
AT THE ACROPOLIS
SUMMER SOLSTICE AT SUNSET
42 COLBY POSTER PRINTING CO., 1332 W. 12th Pl., L.A. 90015 (213) 747-5108

★ SLOW AND STEADY WINS THE RACE ★
PRESENTS

GRACE JONES & DOLLY PARTON

★ ★ ★ ★ ★ DUET ★ ★ ★ ★ ★

ALSO PERFORMING

BAD BRAINS

AT THE ROYAL ALBERT HALL
KENSINGTON GORE, KENSINGTON, LONDON SW7 2AP
December 31, 11pm 2019

4:30 PM, FEBRUARY 29TH
FRANZ
LISZT
CECIL
TAYLOR
LITTLE
RICHARD
AT THE
PARKSIDE LOUNGE

CHARLIE POOLE
PRETTY BAD GIRLS
★★★★★ WITH SPECIAL GUEST ★★★★★
MOTÖRHEAD
April 24, 1965 8pm
at the Avalon Ballroom
1268 Sutter St
San Francisco, California
42 COLBY POSTER PRINTING CO., 1332 W. 12th Pl., L.A. 90015 (213) 747-5108

KING DIAMOND
KING TUBBY
G-DRAGON
(IN THE WOMB VIA CONTACT MIC ON HIS MOTHERS STOMACH)
AHMED
"MAGICIAN OF VOICE"
RUSHDI
★ ★ ★ ★ ★ ★ ★ ALSO ★ ★ ★ ★ ★ ★ ★ ★
VIA LIVE VIDEO STREAM
NICO'S FATAL BICYCLE ACCIDENT
AND THE SIMULTANEOUS
CONCEPTION OF BABY ZHANG
★ ★ ★ ★ ★ ★ ★ ★ ★ ★ ★ ★ ★ ★ ★ ★
NYE'S POLONAISE ROOM
112 EAST HENNEPIN AVENUE
MINNEAPOLIS MINNESOTA
JULY 8TH 1988
42 COLBY POSTER PRINTING CO., 1332 W. 12th Pl., L.A. 90015 (213) 747-5108

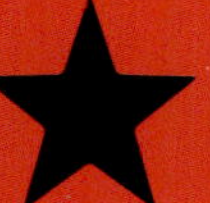

Roulette presents
PLAYING TOGETHER FOR THE FIRST TIME
MARTIN DENNY
TAKEHISA KOSUGI
YMA SUMAC
IANNIS XENAKIS
LIVE
8 PM JAN 11
ROULETTE
509 Atlantic Ave, Brooklyn, NY
917 267 0363

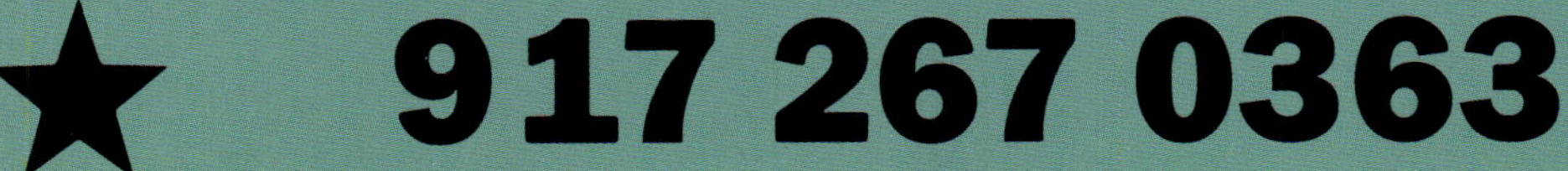

42 COLBY POSTER PRINTING CO., 1332 W. 12th Pl. L.A. 90015 (213) 747-5108

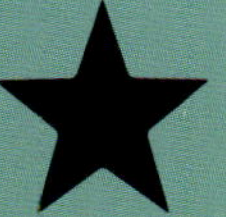

COIL
TERRY MELCHER
INFEST
DRIVIN N CRYIN
BODY COUNT
HOT TUNA
SCRAWL
MARCH 30 ★ 1988 ★ 8:00PM
THE WROCKLAGE
Lexington, KY.
COLBY POSTER PRINTING CO. 1332 W. 12th Pl. L.A. 90015 (213) 747-5106

ELMER BERNSTEIN AS
ELMER FUDD PRESENTS
TOM
★ AND ★
JERRY
(TOM JONES & JERRY GARCIA)
★★★★★★★★★★★ LIVE ★★★★★★★★★★★
AT THE CORNER OF 53RD AND 3RD
RIGHT NOW
WITH YOGI BERRA AS
MASTER OF CEREMONIES,
YOGI BEAR
42 COLBY POSTER PRINTING CO., 1332 W. 12th Pl., L.A. 90015 (213) 747-5108

★ MIDNIGHT TO 6AM ★
NOV 5TH
CHUCK BERRY PRESENTS
BLACK BANANAS
SILVER APPLES
TANGERINE DREAM
AGENT ORANGE
STRAWBERRY ALARM CLOCK
FRESH BLUEBERRY PANCAKE
PEACHES
COLOURED BALLS
RALPH'S ON SUNSET BLVD LOS ANGELES
42 COLBY POSTER PRINTING CO., 1332 W. 12th Pl., L.A. 90015 (213) 747-5108

★★★★ ★ Acéphale presents ★ ★★★★

SUPER
RAIL
BAND
ORCHESTRE DU BUFFET
HÔTEL DE LA GARE DE BAMAKO
MAGMA
THE FREESTYLE BAND
★ Stade Vélodrome
Marseille, France ★
NOVEMBER 11TH 5:55 PM

SPACEMAN
& THE KIWIS
TV ON THE RADIO
YEAH YEAH YEAHS
SEX PISTOLS
GANG OF FOUR
STEVE REICH
★★★★★★★★★★ LIVE AT ★★★★★★★★★★
UNION POOL
484 UNION AVE, BROOKLYN, NY
SEPTEMBER 28
COLBY POSTER PRINTING CO., 1332 W. 12th Pl., L.A. 90015 (213) 747-5108

The MoCo, Montpellier and the
Altermodern Conspiration Society present

CAN
23 SKIDOO
LA CONFIRMATION
DANIELE LUPPI &
PARQUET COURTS
CHICO SCIENCE & NAÇAO ZUMBI
★★★★★★ WITH SPECIAL GUEST ★★★★★★
THE APATHY BAND
April 13th 9:50pm sharp
AT THE MONTPELLIER CONTEMPORAIN
Montpellier, France

MORTON FELDMAN
ON A LEAKY FAUCET
FRED ASTAIRE
PLAYING THE SPOONS AND PREPARED PIANO
WITH
HARPO
PLAYING THE BARBED WIRE HARP
While a landfill is being filled with 1000s of Rolling Stones and Iggy Pop records and cemented over.
VISUALS BY
ERNIE KOVACS
MIDDAY
AT IBERIA RESTAURANT
AND LANDFILL ON FERRY ST. NEWARK, NJ
COLBY POSTER PRINTING CO., 1332 W. 12th Pl., L.A. 90015 (213) 747-5108

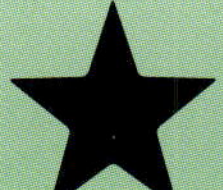
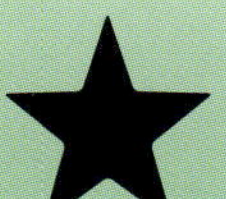

THE NEPENTHE CENTER OF TIME TRAVEL PRESENTS
WHITNEY HOUSTON
PERFORMING A CAPPELLA
SONOROUS TONES SUPERGROUP
FEATURING
WANYA FROM BOYZ II MEN
JAMES RAINBIRD
LAURYN HILL
AND CAT POWER
★★★★★★★ LIVE AT ★★★★★★★★
SÖNGHELLIR (AKA THE CAVE OF SONG) AT SNÆFELLSNES
FEBRUARY 13 AT 2:13PM
42 COLBY POSTER PRINTING CO. 1332 W. 12th Pl., L.A. 90015 (213) 747-5108

BARNABUS REX PUBLISHING VENTURES PRESENTS

HECTOR LAVOE Y SU ORQUESTRA

WITH OS TINCOÃS

SPECIAL GUEST: CORY DAYE

KIP HANRAHAN AS MASTER OF CEREMONIES

VALENTINE'S DAY

AT THE PALLADIUM, 14TH ST

SUNDAY MORNING TOO EARLY FOR CHURCH!

42 COLBY POSTER PRINTING CO., 1332 W. 12th Pl. L.A. 90015 (213) 747-5108

OPENING CEREMONY PRESENTS:

EMOTIONS ARE TAKING OVER TOUR

INTRODUCTION BY COLIN KAEPERNICK

★ MAZZY STAR ★ ELIZABETH FRASER ★

★ WHITNEY HOUSTON ★ AALIYAH ★

★ KATE BUSH ★ PRISCILLA CHAN ★ ANITA MUI ★

WITH AN OPENING PERFORMANCE BY
BOB MARLEY

Q & A WITH BERNIE SANDERS

CENTRAL PARK STAGE
8/8 at 8pm

COLBY POSTER PRINTING CO. 1332 W. 12th Pl. L.A. 90015 (213) 747-5105

CLUB FUCK PRESENTS

★ ★

JONI MITCHELL
Pauline Oliveros

★ ★ ★ ★ ★ ★ ★ ★ WITH ★ ★ ★ ★ ★ ★ ★ ★

FREDERIC
RZEWSKI

ZEITKRATZER

Go-go Dancer, Thomas Crow

★ ★ ★ ★ ★ ★ ★ ★ ★ ★ ★ ★ ★ ★ ★ ★ ★ ★ ★ ★

PERKINS PALACE

129 No. Raymond Avenue,
Pasadena, California

July 15, 8pm

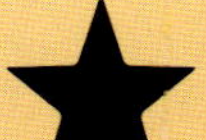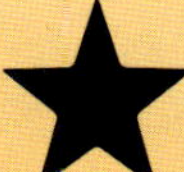

Anger Management presents

BOWIE AND DESMOND DEKKER

PERFORMING TOGETHER

★ WITH SPECIAL GUEST ★

PETER TOSH

speaking to us about the state of the world

★ WITH A WARM UP FEATURING ★

FUGAZI

Pinchers

AND TRIXIE WHITLEY ON DRUMS

★ AT THE ★

Kingston Coronation Market

NOON THIRTY SHARP

★ **AUGUST 25TH** ★

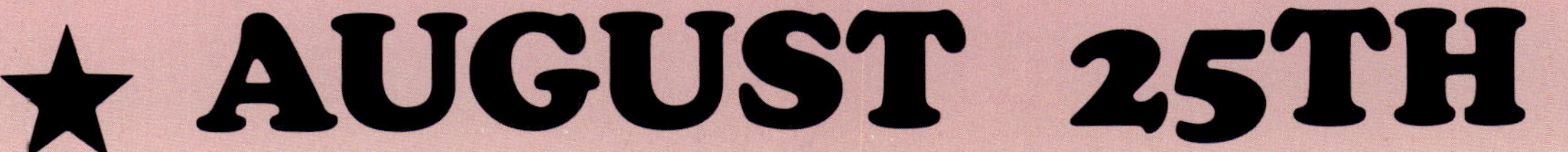

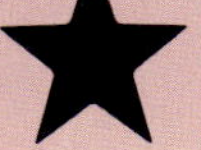

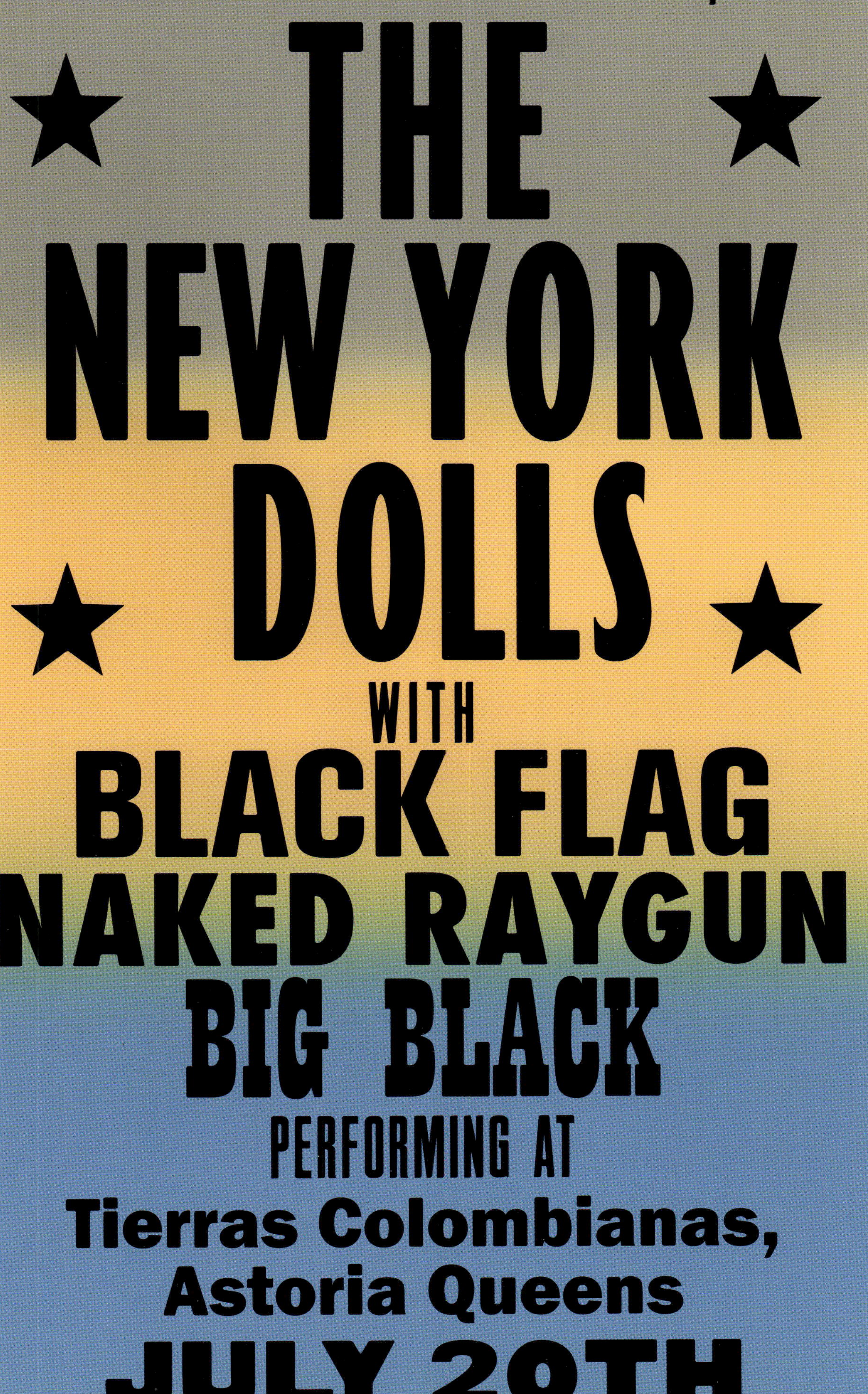

The Colombian Mission to the United Nations presents
THE
NEW YORK
DOLLS
WITH
BLACK FLAG
NAKED RAYGUN
BIG BLACK
PERFORMING AT
Tierras Colombianas,
Astoria Queens
JULY 20TH
COLBY POSTER PRINTING CO., 1332 W. 12th Pl., L.A. 90015 (213) 747-5108

FOLERIO PRESENTS:
BRUCE HAACK
MORT GARSON
STARK REALITY
THE TONY WILLIAMS LIFETIME
SILVER APPLES
★ ★ ★ ★ ★ ★ With special guest ★ ★ ★ ★ ★ ★ ★
WHITE NOISE
OCTOBER 8TH, 1969
★ ★ ★ ★ ★ ★ AT THE ★ ★ ★ ★ ★ ★
CIRCLE STAR THEATER
2 Circle Star Way, San Carlos, CA
42 COLBY POSTER PRINTING CO., 1332 W. 12th Pl., L.A. 90015 (213) 747-5108

M.A.P.S. presents
A BLISSFUL AND TRANSFORMATIONAL EVENING WITH
LANG ELLIOTT
JOAN LA BARBARA
DAPHNE ORAM
OSKAR SALA
HENRY JACOBS
CATHERINE RIBEIRO
GORDON MONAHAN
DJ SETS BY
YAMATAKA EYE
STARTING AT NOON,
DECEMBER 21ST
Littlefield Concert Hall
at Mills College in Oakland, Ca.
42 COLBY POSTER PRINTING CO., 1332 W. 12th Pl. L.A. 90015 (213) 747-5108

ARIEL PRESENTS
BUTTHOLE SURFERS
BEACH BOYS
CRYSTAL WATERS
Performing live
ON THE
PRINCESS CRUISE SHIP
at
14.5994° S, 28.6731° W
June 8th
COLBY POSTER PRINTING CO. 1332 W. 12th Pl. L.A. 90015 (213) 747-5108

Neil deGrasse Tyson presents
A VIEWING OF
COSMOS
with
STEVE MONITE
& FRANK OCEAN
with special guest
AALIYAH
AT THE MCDONALD OBSERVATORY
FORT DAVIS, TX
APRIL 22, EARTH DAY
COLBY POSTER PRINTING CO. 1332 W. 12th Pl., L.A. 90015 (213) 747-5108

★★★★ Tyrannocyrus presents ★★★★
LIL WAYNE &
FREDDIE MERCURY
★★★★★★★ LIVE IN CONCERT ★★★★★★★
WITH SPECIAL GUEST
LES RITA MITSOUKO
★★★★★★★★★ on the ★★★★★★★★★
CHAMPS-ÉLYSÉES,
PARIS, FRANCE
MIDNIGHT
JULY 14TH, 2010
COLBY POSTER PRINTING CO., 1332 W. 12th Pl., L.A. 90015 (213) 747-5108

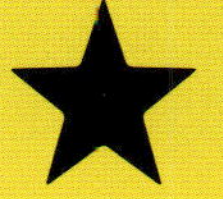

TINY TIM
LITTLE EVA
BIGGIE SMALLS
MEDIUM MEDIUM
LARGE MARGE
BIG BILL BROONZY
GENTLE GIANT
at the
ZIPPER CONCERT HALL
200 SOUTH GRAND AVE.
Los Angeles, CA 90012
COLBY POSTER PRINTING CO., 1332 W. 12th PL. L.A. 90015 (213) 747-5108

MORDE HICKOK AND TIM HORTON'S PRESENT
TONETTA
JONATHAN HALPER
PERFORMS "PUCE MOMENT"
FEATURING MICHIO KURIHARA
ON REVERSE GUITAR
+ THE MONTRÉAL SYMPHONY ORCHESTRA
PLAYS PHILIP GLASS'
SCORE TO "CANDYMAN"
STADE OLYMPIQUE, MONTRÉAL
JULY 1, 10PM
42 COLBY POSTER PRINTING CO., 1332 W. 12th Pl., L.A. 90015 (213) 747-5108

CONTRIBUTORS

Laura Albert, Tim Barnes, Hisham Baroocha, Julianna Barwick, Brian Belott, Sonic Boom, Nicolas Bourriaud, Joe Bradley, Sarah Braman and Phil Grauer, AA Bronson, Andrianna Campbell, Yann Chevallier, Cathy Cho, Larry Clark, Dan Colen, Ani Cordero and Chris Verene, Matthew Patterson Curry, Mike D, Josh Diamond, Andres Santo Domingo, Jim Drain and Kate McNamara, Josh Druckman, Ken Freedman, Sasha Frere-Jones, Delia Gonzales, Andrew Guenther, Tom Hall, Elizabeth Hart, Bob James, Chris Johanson & Jo Jackson, Pali Kashi and Sarah Elliot, Steve Lafreniere, Noah Lennox, JT LeRoy, Carol Lim and Humberto Leon, Arto Lindsay, Justin Lowe and Jonah Freeman, Lydia Lunch, Paul Major, Carlo McCormick, Phil Manley, Christian Marclay, Martin Maugeais, Dave Muller, Hans-Ulrich Obrist, Yoko Ono, Mike Osterhout, Tony Oursler, Peanut Butter Wolf, Michael Pestel, Ara Peterson, Mary Ping, Abby Portner, Stephen Prina, Rob Pruitt, Quasimoto, Mariah Robertson and Jackie Klempay, Jeff Ryan, Ryan Schreiber, Peter Schumann / Bread & Puppet Theater, Martha and Richard Shaw with Alice Shaw, Josh Smith, Mike Sniper, Agathe Snow, Space Lady, D. Charles Speer, Haim Steinbach and Gwen Smith, Peter Sutherland and Maia Ruth Lee, Matt Sweeney, Spencer Sweeney, Carter Thornton, Mikey Turner and Clark Griffin, Tunde Whitten, Michael Williams, Hyla Willis, Terry Winters, Rich Zerbo.

IMAGINARY CONCERTS:
VOLUME TWO

Imaginary Concerts, 2008 - 2018, by Peter Coffin
Untitled (Designs for Colby Poster Co.), 2008
Copyright © Peter Coffin

Poster typesetting and publication design
by Adam Turnbull for Pacific

First Edition, ARC 059
ISBN: 978-1-944860-17-2
Library of Congress Control Number: 2017958054

Printed in China through Asia Pacific Offset

Special Thanks to Imaginary Concert contributors,
Glenn Hinman at The Colby Poster Printing Company,
Michael Benevento, Adam Turnbull, Carlo McCormick,
Keith Gray and Max Schumann at Printed Matter,
Andres Santo Domingo, Jesse Pollock, Casey Whalen
and Thomas Clapp at Anthology Editions.

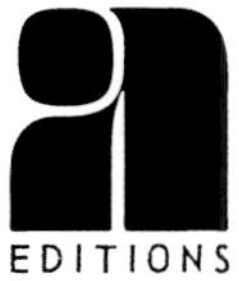

Anthology Editions
87 Guernsey Street
Brooklyn, NY 11222

anthologyeditions.com